TOP TEN LONGEST

Ben Hubbard

Asia

D0519436

Publisher: Melissa Fairley
Art Director: Faith Booker
Editor: Victoria Garrard
Designer: Emma Randall
Production Controller: Ed Green
Production Manager: Suzy Kelly

ISBN: 978 1 84898 209 3

Picture credits (t=top; b=bottom; c=centre; l=left; r=right; OFC=outside front cover):
Tomas Bravo/Reuters: 16, 17, 29tr. Image(s) courtesy of Martin Strel (www.amazonswim.com): 20–21, 29bl.
FilmMagic/Getty Images: 5t, 6, 8, 28tr, 28bl. Getty Images: 21t, 22–23, 28bl, 29cl. Ingrid Grillo-Willis: 27t. M. Robert
Knight/Rex Features: 13. Krishnan/Ardea.com: 4, 10–11, 28br. Ranald Mackechnie/Guinness World Records: 9.
Joe McDonald/Corbis: OFC. The Natural History Museum, London: 14. Shutterstock: 1, 2, 7 both, 14–15, 18–19, 19t,
24–25, 27b, 28tl, 29cr, 29br. Time & Life Pictures/Getty Images: 26. Unimedia Images/Rex Features: 5b, 12–13, 29tl.

Thank you to Lorraine Petersen and the members of nasen

Every effort has been made to trace copyright holders, and we apologize in advance for any omissions.
We would be pleased to insert the appropriate acknowledgements in any subsequent edition of this publication

NOTE TO READERS
The website addresses are correct at the time of publishing. However, due to the ever-changing
nature of the internet, websites and content may change. Some websites can contain links that
are unsuitable for children. The publisher is not responsible for changes in content or website
addresses. We advise that internet searches should be supervised by an adult.

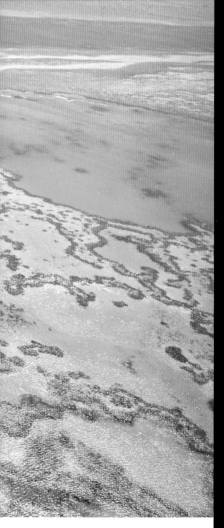

The Great Barrier Reef, Australia

CONTENTS

INTRODUCTION

This book is all about the world's longest things.

From long creatures...

...to long fingernails...

...to the longest car on Earth.

At ten metres long, the reticulated python is the longest snake in the world.

Lee Redmond holds the Guinness World Record for the longest fingernails for a female.

Jay Ohrberg's 26-wheel limousine is the world's longest car.

LONGEST LEGS

The longest legs in the world belong to a Russian woman called Svetlana Pankratova.

Svetlana's legs are 132 centimetres long. That's almost twice the length of the shortest man in the world. He Pingping is only 74.61 centimetres tall!

Svetlana is 196 centimetres tall and has size 11 feet.

"It's challenging to travel on planes. I don't have enough legroom."
Svetlana Pankratova

Long-legged creatures

The daddy longlegs, or pholcidae spider, has a tiny body and very long legs.

Body: two to ten millimetres

Legs: up to 30 millimetres

The ostrich has the longest legs of any bird. Their legs can be up to 150 centimetres long!

LONGEST FINGERNAILS

Some people go to extreme lengths to set records.

Lee Redmond didn't cut her fingernails for 30 years. Her longest nail was 90 centimetres and all her nails measured a total of 8.65 metres.

She holds the world record for longest female fingernails. But at the beginning of 2009, Lee was in a car accident. She wasn't badly hurt, but did lose her nails.

Melvin Booth holds the record for the longest nails on a male pair of hands. His nails measure 9.05 metres.

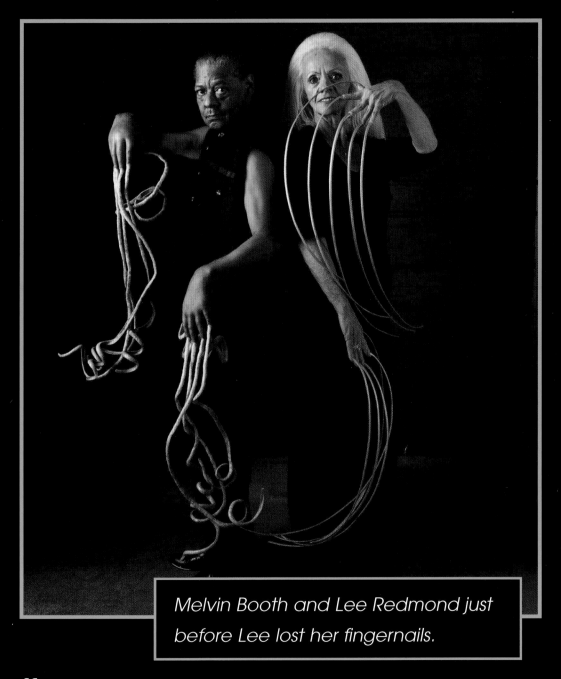

Melvin Booth and Lee Redmond just before Lee lost her fingernails.

"I feel so much lighter without my fingernails. I won't grow them again."
Lee Redmond

LONGEST REPTILE

The reticulated python is the longest snake in the world. It can be up to ten metres in length.

That's more than five grown men lying in a line, head to toe.

The python has curved teeth to bite its prey with. These teeth hold the animal still, while the snake squeezes it to death. Then it devours the animal whole – no chewing needed!

LONGEST CAR

Celebrities love to be seen getting out of limousines.

The longer the better!

Jay Ohrberg from California, USA, decided to go one step further. He built a limousine 30.5 metres long. That's about half the length of a football field.

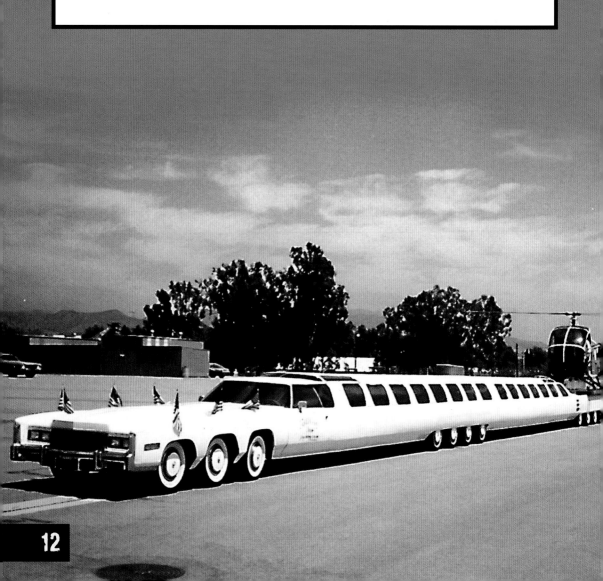

The limousine has:
- 26 wheels
- a Jacuzzi
- a sun deck
- a king-sized bed
- a swimming pool (with diving board)
- a helipad!

Jay has also designed a very long stretch Ferrari. Look out for more of Jay's creations in films such as *Batman Returns* and *Back to the Future*.

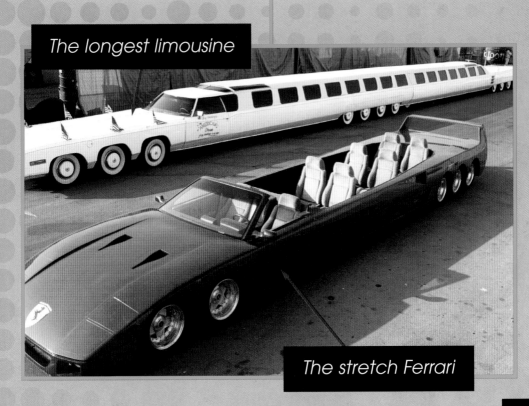

The longest limousine

The stretch Ferrari

LONGEST INSECT

Chan's megastick is the world's longest insect. A new species of stick insect, it measures 56.7 centimetres long.

A speciman of Chan's megastick is kept in the Natural History Museum in London.

Chan's megastick was discovered in a Borneo rainforest in 2008.

Chan's megastick

Stick insects blend into the background and are very hard to spot. This camouflage protects them from predators.

LONGEST HOTDOG

If you love hotdogs, how about
a visit to Monterrey, Mexico?

In 2008 the world's longest hotdog was made
in Monterrey. It was 114.32 metres long. That's
longer than a football field.

*The hotdog is measured by
Guinness World Records.*

First the bread was sliced open with a surgeon's scalpel. Then the sausage was put in and sprayed with mustard.

Finally, it was chopped into 1,000 pieces and handed out to the people watching.

LONGEST LIVING ORGANISM

The Great Barrier Reef is in the Coral Sea off the Australian coast. The reef is made up of billions of organisms, called coral polyps.

The reef is 2,000 kilometres long which makes it the longest coral reef in the world. It is also the longest structure made by living organisms.

The reef is made of 2,900 individual reefs and 71 coral islands.

Four hundred species of coral can be found on the reef. It is also home to many endangered species, including the sea turtle.

Coral

Reef

The Great Barrier Reef is so big it can be seen from space!

LONGEST SWIM

In 2007 Martin Strel completed the longest swim in history.

He swam the Amazon river in South America – all 5,268 kilometres of it!

Martin swam ten hours a day, for 66 days to finish.

The Amazon is a dangerous river, containing bullsharks, anacondas and crocodiles.

As he swam, Martin was attacked by flesh-eating piranhas and stung by wasps.

"For me it was about achieving the impossible, like Hillary reaching the top of Everest."
Martin Strel

LONGEST SHIP

The *Emma Maersk* is the longest ship in the world at 397 metres. That's nearly four football fields long.

This "megaship" is also the largest container ship in the world. It can carry thousands of tonnes of cargo.

Despite her heavy load, the *Emma Maersk* has a crew of only 13 people. It can travel at a very impressive 48 kilometres per hour.

LONGEST MAN-MADE STRUCTURE

The Great Wall of China is the longest man-made structure in the world.

It was built to defend the Chinese Empire from its enemies.

The Great Wall is a massive 7,300 kilometres long!

The wall was made at a price, however. Often prisoners were sentenced to hard labour constructing the wall. Many people died while building it.

LONGEST LIFESPANS

Frenchwoman Jeanne Louise Calment was born in 1875 and died in 1997.

That's the longest recorded lifespan of any human – 122 years and 164 days.

Jeanne proved age doesn't have to be a barrier. She:

- Rode a bicycle until the age of 100
- Ate around 36 small bars of chocolate a week
- Used olive oil as face cream.

"If you can't do anything about it, don't worry about it."
Jeanne Louise Calment

The longest living land animal was Tu'i Malila,
a tortoise. It lived from 1777 to 1965. That's 188 years!

Tu'i Malila

A Quahog clam

Scientists believe a clam lived between 405 and 410 years – the longest lifespan ever recorded! The Quahog clam was found off the coast of Iceland in 2007. Scientists counted the rings on its shell to work out its age.

TOP TEN LONGEST

Some of the longest things on Earth were created by nature.

Others were built (or grown) by humans.

They are all amazing record breakers.

10

Longest insect:

Chan's megastick,
56.7 centimetres

9

Longest fingernail:

Lee Redmond,
90 centimetres

8

Longest legs:

Svetlana Pankratova,
132 centimetres

7

Longest reptile:

Reticulated python,
ten metres

6

Longest car:

Ohrberg limousine,
30.5 metres

5

Longest hotdog:

Monterrey, Mexico,
114.32 metres

4

Longest ship:

Emma Maersk,
397 metres

3

Longest living organism:

Great Barrier Reef,
2,000 kilometres

2

Longest swim:

Martin Strel,
5,268 kilometres

1

Longest man-made structure:

Great Wall of China,
7,300 kilometres

NEED TO KNOW WORDS

anaconda A snake mostly found in water that kills its prey by suffocating it to death.

camouflage Colourings or markings on an animal that help it hide or blend in with its surroundings.

devour To eat something quickly and hungrily.

drysuit A one-piece suit used to protect the wearer against cold water. Unlike a wetsuit, a drysuit does not let any water in.

endangered When there are not many of an animal left, and the remaining animals are in danger of being hunted or losing their habitat.

helipad A takeoff and landing area for helicopters.

Jacuzzi A hot bath with jets of water, also called a spa pool or hot tub.

lifespan The length of time a human or animal lives for.

megaship A very large ship used for transporting oil and other liquids in large quantities.

polyps Coral animals that have hard outer skeletons that join together. When a polyp dies, its skeleton stays as part of the reef, so the reef keeps on getting bigger and bigger.

predator Animals that hunt and kill other animals for food.

prey An animal caught or hunted for food.

scalpel A small but extremely sharp knife used by surgeons.

specimen An individual animal or plant that is used to study the rest of the species.

LONGEST RECORD BREAKERS

- The Pororoca wave in Brazil is the most dangerous tidal wave in the world. In 2003, Picuruta Salazar rode the Pororoca for 37 minutes. The wave carried him 59.5 kilometres.

- In 2003, Erin Hemmings threw an Aerobie ring 406 metres in San Francisco. It stayed in the air for 30 seconds.

- Tom Sietas held his breath for 17 minutes and 19 seconds in 2008, setting the world record.

FIND OUT MORE ONLINE

http://www.guinnessworldrecords.com/

http://www.chesterzoo.org/AnimalsandPlants/

Reptiles/Snakes/ReticulatedPython.aspx

http://www.emma-maersk.info

http://www.greatwall-of-china.com

http://www.amazonswim.com/main.php

INDEX